LIVING IN AFRICA

Living in
NIGERIA

Annabelle Lynch

FRANKLIN WATTS
LONDON • SYDNEY

Franklin Watts
First published in Great Britain in 2016 by The Watts Publishing Group

Credits
Series Editor: Julia Bird
Editor: Sarah Silver
Series Design: D.R. ink

ISBN 978 1 4451 4865 6

Picture credits: Irene Abdou/Alamy: 10t, 18b. A.F. Archive/Alamy: 17t. agafapaperiapunta/istockphoto: 16t. AGIF/Shutterstock: 17b. Christian Bertrand/Shutterstock: 16b. bonchan/Shutterstock: 21c. Lucian Coman/Shutterstock: 12t. Gary Cook/Alamy: 9b, 19t. Education Images/UIG/Getty Images: front cover. Pius Utomi Ekpei/AFP/GettyImages: 15t. EPA/Alamy: 21b. EyeUbiquitous/Superstock: 6t, 8b, 10b. Mike Goldwater/Alamy: 8t. Johnny Greig/istockphoto: 19b. Igor Groshev/Dreamstime: 11b. Robert Harding PL/Alamy: 21t. Robert Harding PL/Superstock: 20t. Anton Ivanov/Shutterstock: 4t. Sergei Kostin /Dreamstime: 13t. Lorimer Images/Shutterstock: 7t, 14t, 22b. Licinia Machado/Shutterstock: 19c. Alexander Mychko/Dreamstime: 15b. Maks Narodenko/Shutterstock: 14b. Orokiet/Alamy: 12b. redpip1894/Shutterstock: 11t. Ferdinand Reus/Dreamstime: 18t. Feije Riemersma/Dreamstime: 5t. RooMtheAgency/Alamy: 5b. Paul D Smith/Shutterstock: 14c. Smithore/istockphoto: 17c. Stuart Taylor/Dreamstime: 13b. Peeter Vlisimaa/istockphoto: 6b, 7b, 9t. Willeyj/Dreamstime: 20b.

Printed in China

MIX
Paper from
responsible sources
FSC® C104740

Franklin Watts
An imprint of
Hachette Children's Group
Part of The Watts Publishing Group
Carmelite House
50 Victoria Embankment
London EC4Y 0DZ

An Hachette UK Company
www.hachette.co.uk

www.franklinwatts.co.uk

Contents

Words in bold are in the glossary on page 23.

Welcome to Nigeria

Hello! I live in Nigeria.

Where is Nigeria?

Nigeria is a big country in West Africa. It shares **borders** with four other African countries – Benin, Cameroon, Chad and Niger. It has a long coast along the Gulf of Guinea.

tropical rainforest →

What does Nigeria look like?

In the south, Nigeria has mountains and rich **tropical rainforests.** In the north you can find huge, flat grasslands. In between the two are low hills and scrub known as savannah. The River Niger runs across Nigeria, and gives the country its name.

What's the weather like?

In the tropical south-east, it is hot and wet all year round. Central and west Nigeria have wet and dry seasons, while in the north the weather is hot and often very dry.

A beach near Lagos, in the south

People in Nigeria

I come from Nigeria. People who come from Nigeria are called Nigerian.

Giant of Africa

Nigeria has the biggest **population** of any country in Africa and the seventh biggest population in the world. Around 181 million people live in Nigeria.

An Igbo celebration

Living together

Many of the people living in Nigeria come from groups called tribes. Tribes come from the same place, speak the same language and have the same **culture** and **traditions**. The four biggest tribes in Nigeria are the Igbo, Hausa, Yoruba and Fulani.

Over 520 different languages are spoken in Nigeria!

Nigerian National **Mosque** in Abuja

Religion

Christianity and Islam are the two biggest religions in Nigeria. Around ten per cent of Nigerians follow traditional African religions.

Cities

Around half of people in Nigeria live in the fast-growing cities. I live in the biggest city, Lagos.

Lively Lagos

Lagos is Nigeria's biggest city by far, with around 13 million people living here – and it's still growing fast! Until 1991, Lagos was the **capital** city of Nigeria, and it is still the most important city for business. Found on the Gulf of Guinea, it has a very busy **port**.

Lagos is spread across a collection of islands and the **mainland**.

A street in downtown Abuja

Abuja

Abuja is a **planned city** located in the middle of Nigeria. It is the capital city, and the government meets here. Around 2.5 million people live in Abuja.

Kano

About 3.5 million Nigerians live in the city of Kano in north Nigeria. Kano has a very long history and used to be an important centre for **trade** with North Africa and Europe.

Kano city

What people do

People in Nigeria work in lots of different jobs. Often, the work they do depends on whether they live in the city or the countryside.

City jobs

In Nigeria's cities, many people find jobs in companies, shops or banks. Others work in factories, helping to make food products, clothes or cars.

Women working in a peanut oil factory

Country work

In the countryside, most people work in farming. They grow crops, such as cacao (from which chocolate is made), bananas, beans, maize (corn) and nuts. These crops are sold in Nigeria and all over the world.

maize

Dig it out

Nigeria has a huge wealth of **resources** buried underground. These include oil, **natural gas** and metals, such as gold and tin. Many people work to **mine** these resources so they can be used to power machines or make new products.

An oil rig in Lagos

Wildlife

Nigeria has lots of amazing and rare wildlife. In some places animals are disappearing because their homes are at risk.

Great apes

Rare Cross River gorillas are found deep in the forests near the border with Cameroon. They eat fruit, bark and some bugs. There are only around two or three hundred of these gorillas left in the wild as much of their forest home has been cut down or burned, so you would be very lucky to see one.

Cross River gorilla

Top five rarest animals in Nigeria

1 West African lion
2 Cross River gorilla
3 Cameroonian forest shrew
4 Red-eared guenon (monkey)
5 White-throated guenon

African raven

River creatures

The wetlands of the River Niger are home to flocks of colourful birds, from flamingos to parrots. You can also find different types of fish, crocodiles and even hippopotamuses!

Grassland animals

In the huge, rich grasslands of central Nigeria you can see elephants, lions, leopards and warthogs. Many of these creatures are **hunted** for their tusks, fur or meat, so they are now protected by the government.

leopard

plantain

What we eat

Nigerian food is delicious! We prefer to eat food that is grown locally so that it is always fresh.

fufu

Main meals

Nigerians enjoy eating lots of spicy soups and stews. These are often accompanied with rice, *fufu* (made from a ground root vegetable called cassava) or **plantain**, and piles of beans.

Thanks to its warm climate, fruit grows well in Nigeria. Pineapples, bananas and melons can be eaten almost all year round.

Meat and fish

Skewers of grilled chicken, beef or goat meat called *suya*, are very popular all over Nigeria. They can be bought at street stalls. Nearer the coast, people like to eat spicy seafood stews, made with fish, shrimps and crab.

Famous foods

Jollof rice is one of the most famous Nigerian dishes. It is cooked with onions, tomato and chilli peppers – vegetables, fish and meat can be added too. For a sweet snack or dessert, sugary, fried dough balls called puff puff are very popular.

jollof

Having fun

Music and films are a big part of Nigerian life. We also love playing and watching sport.

Afrobeat

Make music

People love music in Nigeria! The different tribes (see page 7) all have their own traditional music and instruments, such as special drums, horns and trumpets. Some types of Nigerian popular music, such as juju and Afrobeat, have spread around the world.

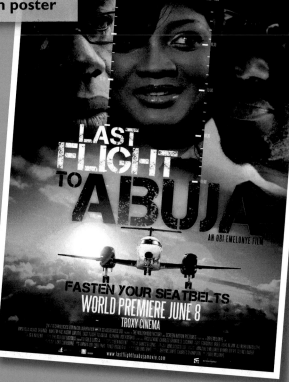

Film

Nigeria has the second biggest film industry in the world. Known as 'Nollywood', it makes around 2,000 new films a year. People can watch them at big cinemas or buy them on DVD from street stalls. Comedies and romances are especially popular!

Ayo is a popular, traditional Nigerian board game. The aim of the game is to collect more seeds from the board than anyone else.

← ayo

Football mad

Football is Nigeria's national sport and the men's and women's teams, known as the Super Eagles, regularly play in international competitions. Nigerian footballers play for clubs all around the world.

The Nigerian men's football team at the 2014 FIFA World Cup

Famous places

Nigeria has some great places to visit, from national parks to sandy beaches.

Rocky wonder

Zuma Rock is one of the most famous sights in Nigeria. It rises 725 m above the ground north of Abuja and has a spooky 'face' on one of its sides. People can climb right to the top of Zuma Rock but be warned – it is very steep!

Can you see the spooky face in Zuma Rock?

Wildlife haven

Yankari National Park is a wonderful place to see Nigerian wildlife, such as elephants, lions and monkeys, up close. Yankari also has a famous, warm **natural spring**, and you can swim in its crystal-clear waters.

Natural spring at Yankari

Elugushi Beach

Elugushi Beach

Nigeria has some beautiful beaches along the Gulf of Guinea. Elugushi is one of the busiest! You can paddle in the waves, build a big sandcastle or even take a pony ride along the golden sands.

Festivals and celebrations

We hold many festivals throughout the year in Nigeria. Some are religious, but many are not. I love dancing at the festivals!

Christian celebrations

In Nigeria, just as in other countries around the world, the two biggest Christian festivals are Christmas and Easter. Nigerians celebrate the life of Jesus Christ with dancing, feasting and drumming and the streets are lit up with bright colours.

Christmas lights in Lagos

Muslim festivals

There are three big Muslim festivals in Nigeria every year – Eid al Maulud, Eid al Fitri and Eid al Kabir. Eid al Maulud marks the birth of the Muslim **prophet** Muhammad (**pbuh**), while Eid al Fitri celebrates the end of **Ramadan**. Eid al Kabir is known as the 'festival of sacrifice' and is often celebrated with traditional horse-riding shows known as durbars.

A durbar in Kano, Nigeria

Celebrating yams

Yams are so important in Nigeria that they have a festival all of their own. People gather together at harvest time to dance, give thanks to the gods and, of course, eat!

Tribal celebrations

The many Nigerian tribes have their own special days. These include the Yoruba festival, Osun, which is held in August every year. People give thanks to the river goddess, Osun, by offering her gifts.

Celebrating the Osun festival

Nigeria: Fast facts

Capital: Abuja

Population: 181 million

Area: 923,768 sq km

Languages: English (official) and many other African languages

Currency: Nigerian Naira

Main religions: Christianity, Islam, traditional religions

Longest river: Niger, 4,200 km

Highest mountain: Chapel Waddi, 2,419 m

National holidays: New Year's Day (1 January), Good Friday, Easter Monday, Labour Day (1-2 May), Democracy Day (29 May), Eid al Fitri, Eid al Kabir, National Day (1 October), Eid al Maulud, Christmas Day (25 December), Boxing Day (26 December)

Glossary

border the boundary that divides two countries

capital the city in which the government of a country meets

culture shared beliefs and traditions

hunt to kill wild animals for food or sport

mainland the main part of a country, rather than the islands around it

mine to dig into the ground for materials, such as oil

mosque the place where Muslims worship

natural gas a gas that can be collected and used as a fuel

natural spring a place where water flows up out of the ground

pbuh short for the Arabic phrase meaning 'peace be upon him'; used after the name of an Islamic prophet to show respect

planned city a city that people planned and built with care

plantain a type of banana used in cooking

population all the people living in a place

port a place by the sea where ships arrive and depart

prophet someone who is believed to speak God's words

Ramadan the ninth month of the Muslim year, where people do not eat between sunrise and sunset

resources things that can be sold for money, such as oil and precious metals

shrew a small animal like a mouse with a long nose

trade to buy and sell goods

tradition something that has been done in the same way for many years

tropical rainforest thick forest found in hot places where it rains a lot

Index